Parham

Introduction

This book is filled with a wonderful variety of activities that have been designed to help children at the first grade level develop the skills and self-confidence they need while learning about God's teachings, the Bible, and Christian values at the same time.

The activities in this book are based on Christian themes and concepts, many of which include Bible verses and stories. Discuss these Christian themes, concepts, verses, and stories with your child to help him or her better understand the important role they play in his or her life.

Curriculum areas covered in this book include phonics, language arts, spelling, art, math, reading, and writing. Skills and concepts featured include following directions, capitalization, punctuation, word identification, identifying parts of a story, consonant blends and digraphs, synonyms and antonyms, alphabetical order, classifying, comparing and contrasting, adding, subtracting, telling time, graphing, and many more.

On pages 68–76 are Christian arts and crafts projects. All materials needed have been listed and encompass everyday objects found in most homes. Guide your child in these projects.

Also included on page 80 is an award you can give your child to motivate him or her or to reward your child for work well done.

You will love watching and helping your child improve many very important skills while he or she learns about God's love for us at the same time!

Name ____

Off to a Good Start

Look at the picture. Say the beginning sound. Fill in the circle next to the beginning letter.

1.

○ d
○ b
○ p

2.
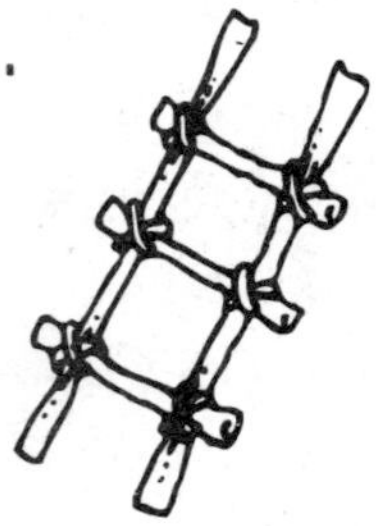
○ t
○ h
○ l

3.

○ w
○ v
○ r

4.

○ m
○ n
○ w

5.

○ b
○ c
○ d

6.
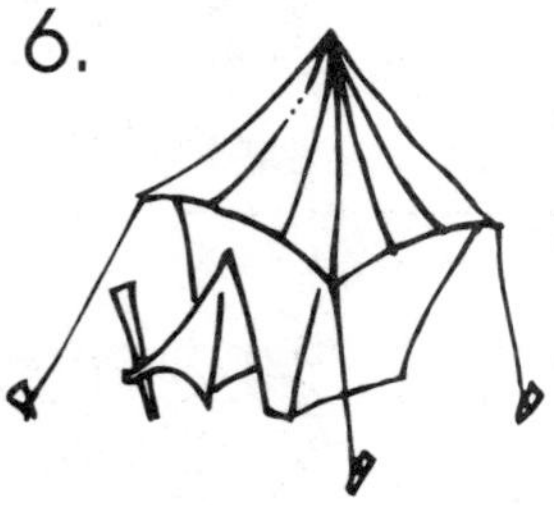
○ f
○ t
○ l

7.

○ h
○ n
○ m

8.
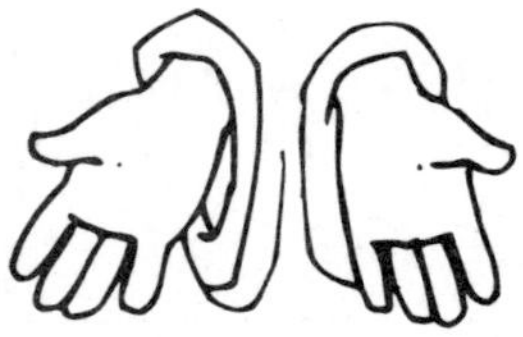
○ n
○ h
○ p

9.

○ w
○ r
○ s

10.

○ r
○ n
○ h

11.

○ h
○ t
○ f

12.

○ c
○ s
○ d

13.
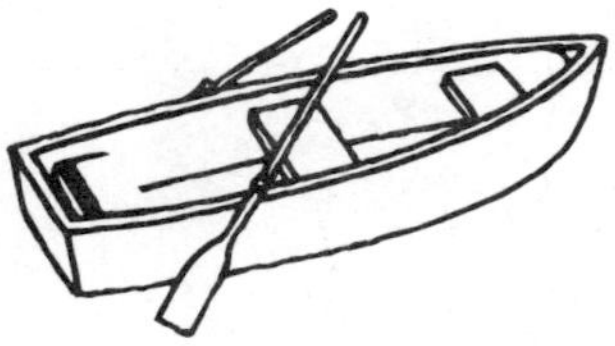
○ c
○ b
○ d

14.

○ p
○ m
○ s

15.

○ b
○ t
○ s

Name ______________________________

Same Sound

Color the two pictures in each row that begin with the same sound.

1. 

2. 

3. 

4. 

5. 

6. 

7. 

Name ____________________

Luke 2:12

A Heaven-sent Sign

Signs along the road help us know we are going in the right direction. What sign did the angel say would help the shepherds find the baby in the town of David? To find the answer, put the first letter of each object in the square provided. Read Luke 2:12 to check your answer!

You will find a 

in 

and lying in a  **.**

Name ____

Who Is Jesus?

Jesus is the ___ ___ ___ ___ ___ of the ___ ___ ___ ___ ___!
1 2 3 4 5 6 7 8 1 9

Match the first letter of each picture below to the numbered line above to finish this name for Jesus.

2

3

6

1

7

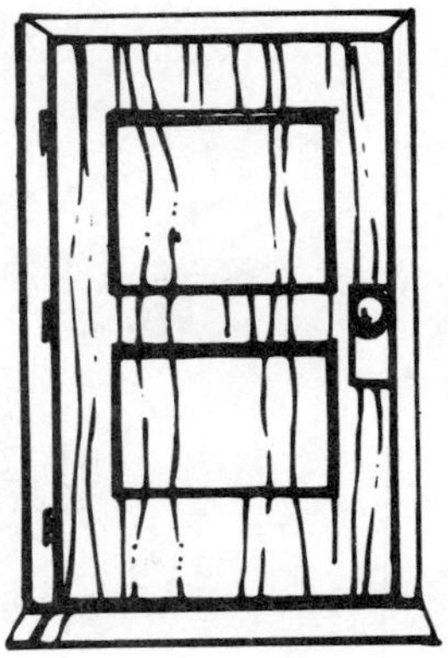
9

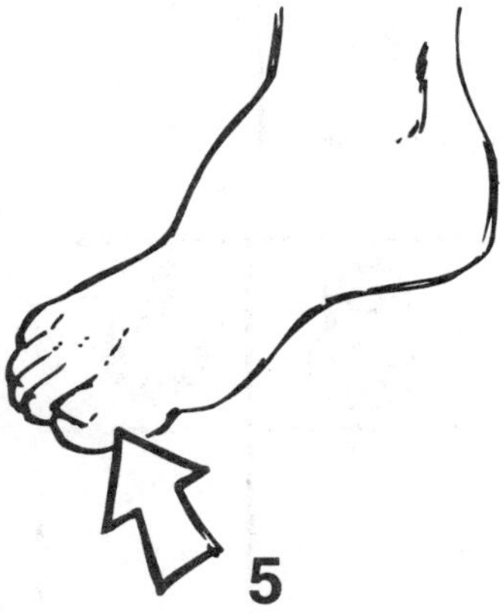
5

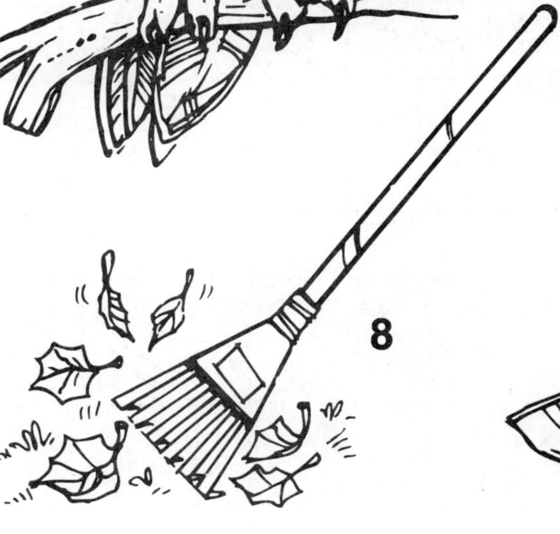
8

4

Name ____________________

In the Beginning

Name each picture. Which blend begins each word? Write **br**, **cr**, **dr**, **fr**, **gr**, **pr**, or **tr**.

1.  ___oss

2.  ___ay

3.  ___own

4.  ___apes

5. 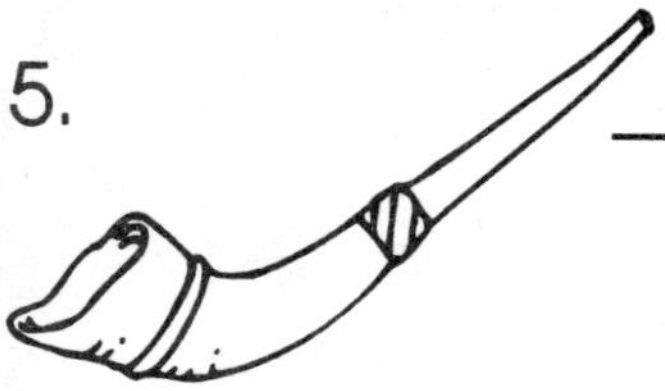 ___umpet

6.  ___og

7.  ___ead

8.  ___anch

9.  ___iends

10.  ___ee

11.  ___um

12.  ___unk

Name ____

Starting Right Off

Look at each picture. Say the beginning sound. Write **ch**, **sh**, or **th**. Then find and circle each word in the puzzle.

1.  ___eep

2.  ___urch

3.  ___ip

4.  ___orn

5.  ___ell

6.  ___ildren

c	h	i	l	d	r	e	n	t
h	c	h	i	y	n	s	s	x
u	s	h	c	h	t	h	h	r
r	h	t	h	o	r	n	e	w
c	i	s	c	t	h	s	e	e
h	p	s	h	e	l	l	p	c

Name ______________________________

What's in the Middle?

What short vowel sound is missing in each word?
Write **a**, **e**, **i**, **o**, or **u**.

1.  s___n

2.  h___nd

3.  f___sh

4.  n___t

5.  p___t

6.  c___t

7.  h___g

8.  l___mp

9.  h___ll

10.  b___ll

11.  f___x

12. 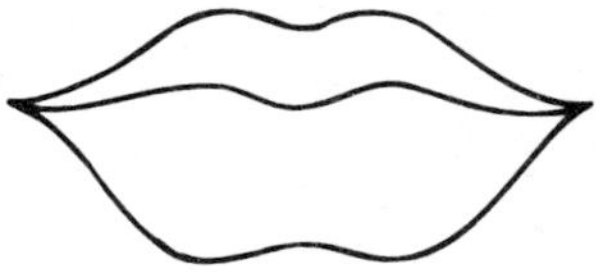 l___ps

Name ____

How Colorful!

Color pictures with . . .

short a—red
short e—blue
short i—green
short o—yellow
short u—purple

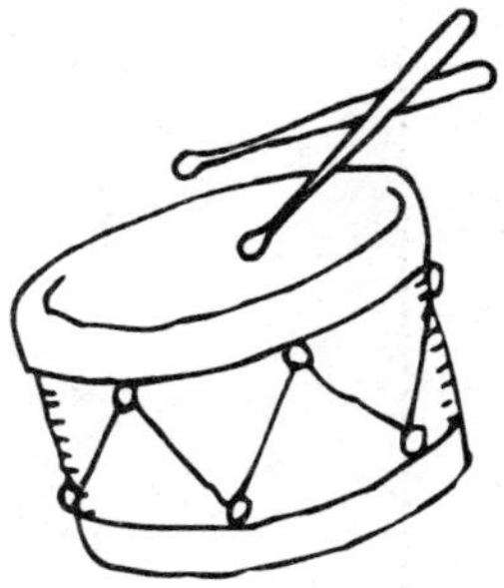

Name ____

Silence Please!

Write the missing long vowel **a**, **i**, **o**, or **u** in the first blank. Write the silent **e** in the second blank.

1.  r___b___

2.  fl___t___

3.  kn___f___

4. 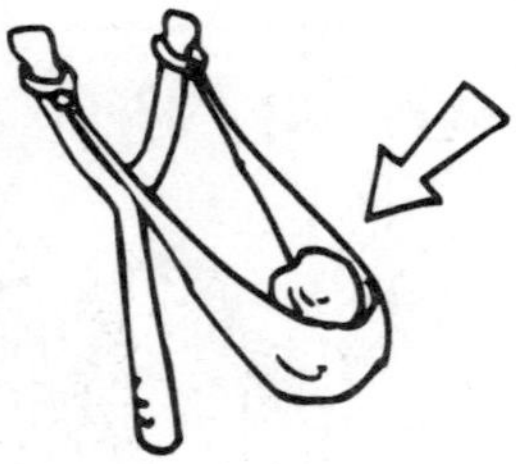 st___n___

5.  g___t___

6.  b___k___

7.  sm___l___

8.  m___l___

9. 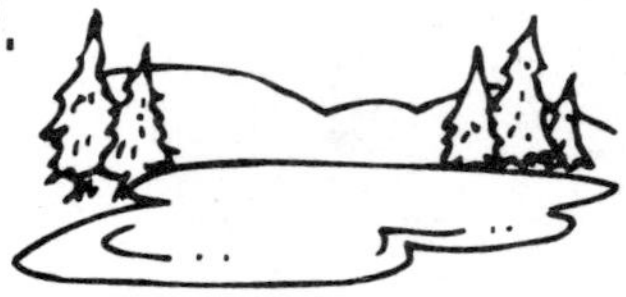 l___k___

10.  r___p___

11.  v___n___

12.  t___m___

Name ____

You Don't Say!

Some words have silent consonants. Say the words. Circle the letters you do not hear.

1. calf

2. kneel

3. sign

4. climb

5. sword

6. write

7. lamb

8. walk

9. mighty

10. wrist

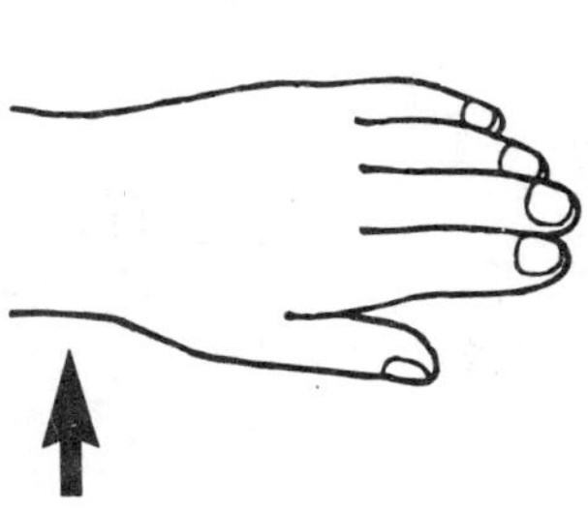

11. knife

12. limb

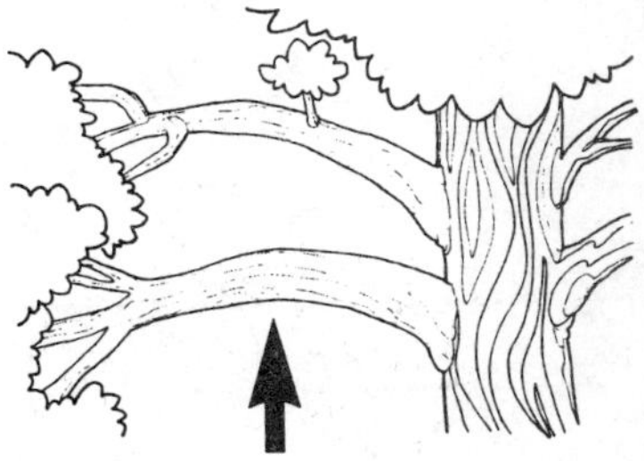

Name ____________________

A Dish of Fish

Say the word for each picture. Then write the word from the box that rhymes.

well	love	day	dish	pan	feed	dark	peep	calf	save	went	coat

1. 
2. 
3. 
4. 
5. 
6. 
7. 
8. 
9. 
10. 
11. 
12. 

Name ______________________________

Another Way to Say *Brave*

Write the word that means the same as the word in **dark** print.

afraid	struck	brave	large
huge	small	lifted	glad

1. Goliath was a very **large** man. ______________
2. God's people were **fearful** of Goliath and did not want to fight him. ______________
3. David was not a **big** shepherd boy. ______________
4. David picked up five **little** stones and his sling. ______________
5. David was a very **bold** boy and knew God would help him. ______________
6. David **raised** his sling and aimed. ______________
7. The stone **hit** Goliath in the forehead and killed him. ______________
8. God's people were **happy**. ______________

Name ______________________________

Right or Wrong

Write the word from the box that is the opposite of each word in **dark** print.

old	love	right	well	far	light

1. Jesus cared about the **young** and the ____________.

2. Jesus said we should not **hate** our enemies but ____________ them.

3. Jesus was able to make **sick** people feel ____________ again.

4. People came from **near** and ____________ to hear Jesus.

5. Jesus' lessons help us to know ____________ from **wrong**.

6. Jesus leads those in **darkness** to the ____________.

Name ____________________

Genesis 6–9

Water, Water Everywhere

Read the story. Find and write all the compound words. Draw a line between the two words that make up each compound word.

God told Noah to build an ark. Noah did as God asked. Soon everything was covered with water. Only Noah, his family, and two of every kind of animal were saved. They would be inside the ark when the rain came. When the rain stopped, everyone left the ark. God said he would never again cover the earth with water. God made a beautiful rainbow as a sign of his promise.

Write four compound words you know.

Name ______________________________

Luke 5:1–11

Going Fishing

Peter and Andrew went fishing. They caught a lot of fish.

Color:

5	fish	red
4	fish	green
6	fish	blue
3	fish	yellow
7	fish	purple
2	fish	orange
1	fish	black
8	fish	brown

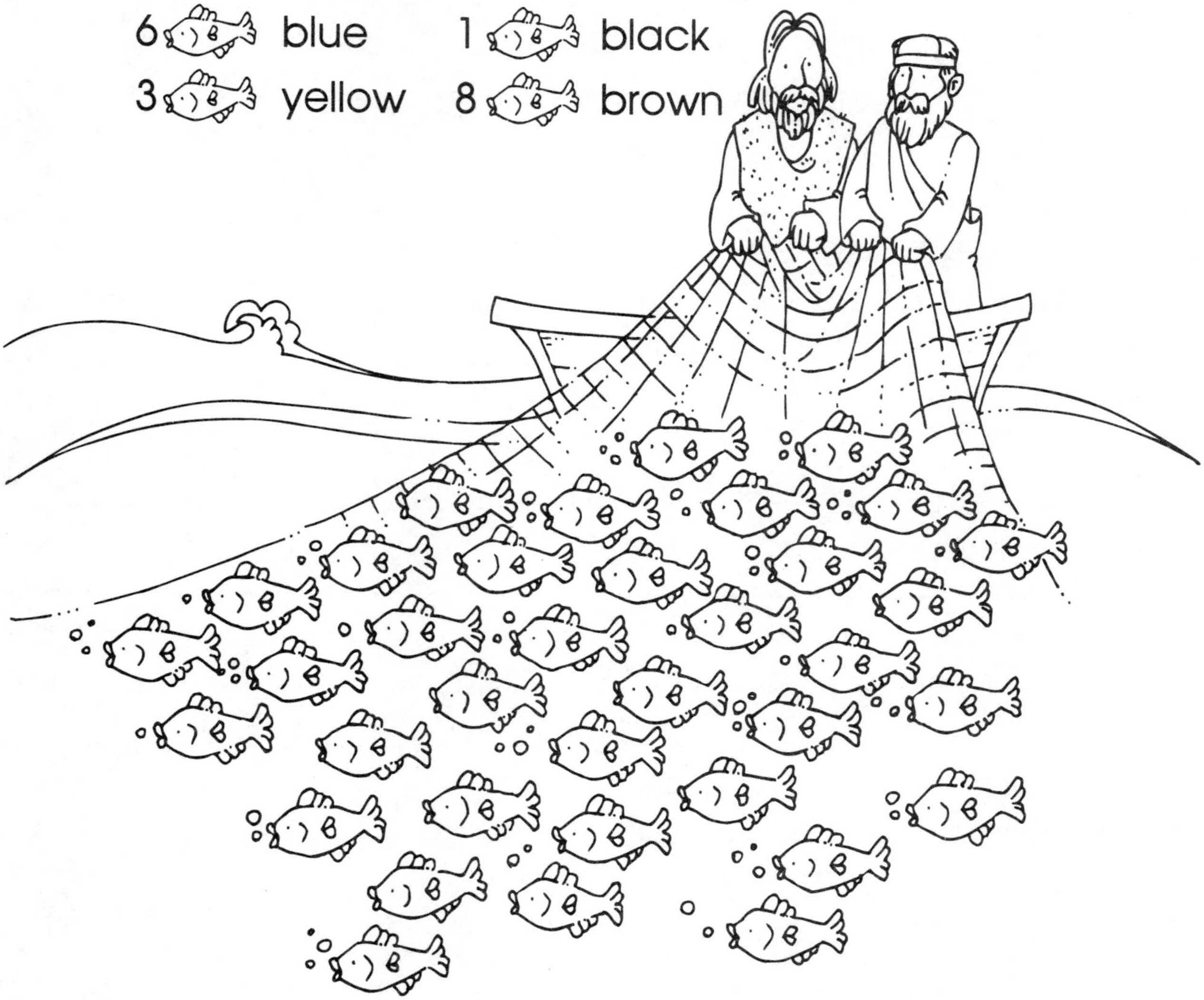

Draw five fish. Color one red, one blue, and three yellow.

Name ____

What's the Word?

Look at each picture. Fill in the circle next to the matching word.

1. 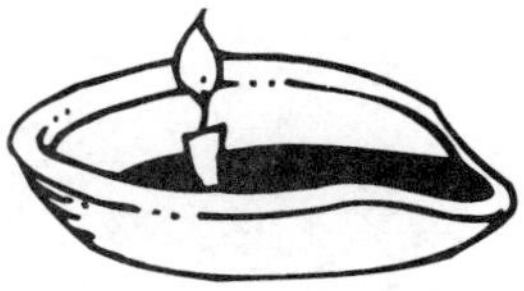
○ lamb
○ lamp
○ comb

2. 
○ crown
○ book
○ cross

3. 
○ came
○ camel
○ goat

4. 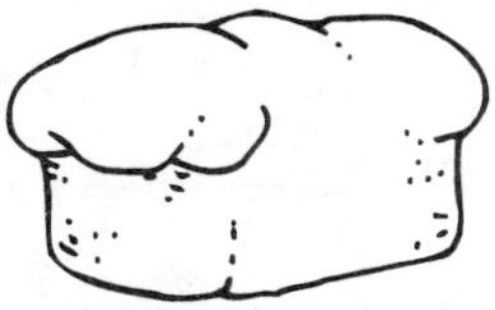
○ bed
○ dead
○ bread

5. 

○ two
○ fish
○ twelve

6. 
○ heart
○ sling
○ sing

7. 
○ wall
○ well
○ bell

8. 
○ bat
○ boat
○ coat

9. 
○ story
○ door
○ star

10. 
○ king
○ kiss
○ run

11. 
○ sheep
○ store
○ dog

12. 
○ cat
○ Bible
○ boat

Name ______________________

Matthew
8:23–27

Jesus, the Wind, and the Sea

Read the story. Write the answers.

Jesus and his disciples were out at sea. A storm came up. The disciples thought the boat might sink. They woke up Jesus. They asked him, "Don't you care if we die?"

Jesus asked why they were afraid. He then told the wind and sea to be quiet and calm.

1. Where were Jesus and his disciples?

____

2. What happened as Jesus slept?

____

3. Why were the disciples afraid?

____

4. What did Jesus ask the disciples?

____

5. What did Jesus do?

____

Name ____

Going to Church

One sentence tells the main idea of each picture. Fill in its circle.

1. ○ The children are learning about Jesus.
   ○ The children are playing.
   ○ The children are in school.

2. ○ Dan has a book.
   ○ Dan is reading his Bible.
   ○ Dan's Bible is new.

3. ○ Martha is a good singer.
   ○ Singing is fun.
   ○ Martha is singing in church.

4. ○ Cal is sad.
   ○ Cal is talking to God.
   ○ Cal is ready for bed.

5. ○ The pastor is reading.
   ○ The pastor is talking about Jesus.
   ○ The pastor is kneeling.

Main idea

Name ______________________________

Learning About Jesus

Fill in the circle of the sentence that tells the main idea of each story.

Maggie wants to know all about Jesus. She reads her Bible every day. She goes to Sunday school. She asks a lot of questions about Jesus.

○ Maggie loves Jesus.

○ Maggie wants to learn about Jesus.

○ Maggie likes to read.

Alex knows that Jesus is the Son of God. Jesus taught others all about God's love. He made sick people well again. He even walked on water.

○ Alex knows many things about Jesus.

○ Alex read about Jesus.

○ Jesus is the Son of God.

Write one thing you know about Jesus.

____

____

Name ______________________________

The Cover Story

Look at the cover of the book. Answer the questions.

The **title** is the name of the book.

The **author** wrote the book.

The **illustrator** drew the pictures.

1. What is the title of the book?

____

2. Who is the author of the book?

____

3. Who is the illustrator of the book?

____

4. Write the name of your favorite book.

____

Name ______________________________

Jonah 1–4

Watch Out for That Whale!

Read the story. Use the words from the box to fill in the blanks.

bad	good	sea	Nineveh
storm	whale	spit	prayed

God told Jonah to go to ______________. The people there were ______________. Jonah was to tell them to be ______________.

Jonah did not want to go. He got on a boat. A ______________ came up. The sailors threw Jonah into the ______________. A ______________ swallowed him. Jonah ______________ and prayed.

The whale ______________ Jonah out on land. Jonah went to Nineveh. The people listened to him. They started being good.

Name ______________________________

What a Character!

Think about your favorite Bible story. Draw a picture of the most important character in that story. Then answer the questions.

1. What is the name of the most important character?

2. What three words do you think best tell about him or her?

3. Why do you think this character is important?

4. Was this character a good or a bad person?

Name ______________________________

Bible People and Places

Draw a line under the special names of people and places. Write the names of the people in ABC order. Write the names of the special places in ABC order.

Mary and Joseph lived in the town of Nazareth in a country called Palestine. The ruler wanted to count everyone in his empire. To do this, people were ordered to go back to their hometowns. Mary and Joseph returned to Bethlehem. It was there that baby Jesus was born.

People	Places
______________	______________
______________	______________
______________	______________

Write the name of a person and a place from the Bible.

____

Name ______________________________

One and More Than One

Write the missing words that match the pictures.

1.  baby  babies

2.  ________ churches 

3.  angel  ________

4.  city  ________

5. _____  lambs 

6.  cross  ________

7.  Bible  ________

Name ______________________________

The Sound of *Y*

In the word *story*, **y** makes the long **e** sound. In the word *try*, **y** makes the long **i** sound.

army

cry

city

sky

baby

fly

Write the words from the box in the correct columns.

y sounds like **e**	**y** sounds like **i**
____________	____________
____________	____________
____________	____________

Write a word that rhymes with **try**.

____

Name ____

Names From the Bible

Write the name to finish each sentence. Begin each name with a capital letter.

Noah	Adam	Jesus	Moses	Eve	David	Jonah

1. The Son of God is ______________ .

2. The man who built the ark was ______________ .

3. Goliath was beaten by ______________ .

4. The first man was ______________ .

5. The first woman was ______________ .

6. The man who led his people out of Egypt was ______________ .

7. God sent a whale to swallow ______________ when he didn't obey God.

Name ____________________

Mark 10:46–52

Jesus and the Blind Man

Write the words in order to make sentences. They will tell a story. Remember, the first word in a sentence begins with a capital letter.

1. the road. sat by man A

2. needed help. He

3. see. He not could

4. walked by. Jesus

5. him Jesus see. made

6. happy. The was man

Name ________________________________

About the Bible

Read each sentence. Write a **.** at the end of each telling sentence. Write a **?** at the end of each asking sentence.

1. We are learning about the Bible ☐

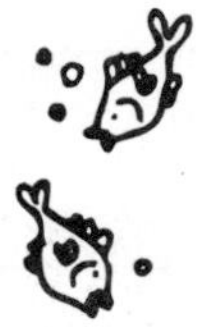

2. It tells about God and his love for us ☐

3. Do you have a Bible ☐

4. Altogether, there are 66 books in the Bible ☐

5. How many books are in the Old Testament ☐

6. Can you name the four Gospels ☐

7. The story of Noah is in the book of Genesis ☐

8. You can read about Jesus in the New Testament ☐

9. Do you read your Bible every day ☐

10. We go to church to learn about the Bible ☐

Name ______________________________

Spelling Words From the Bible

What words from the Bible do you need to practice? Choose at least six. Write them in the puzzle. Write other letters in the extra boxes. Then look for your words and color them. Write the words on the lines.

Write two words from the Bible that you don't know.

Name ______________________________

Plan a Story

Plan a story about yourself and someone from the Bible.

1. List some of the people from the Bible you might like to have in your story.

2. What would you like to happen in your story? Write three ideas. Make a check mark next to the one you like most.

3. Write about something good that happens at the end of your story.

Name ______________________________

Jesus Goes to Jerusalem

Circle the picture that matches each sentence about Jesus.

1. Jesus ate with his disciples.

2. Jesus broke the bread into pieces.

3. Jesus shared the bread with his friends.

4. Jesus took the cup of wine.

5. After supper, Jesus went to pray.

Name ____________________

Weather or Not

Fill in the circle next to the sentence that matches the picture.

1. ○ It has stopped raining.
   ○ It has stopped snowing.

2. ○ It is cold.
   ○ It is warm.

3. ○ There is a strong wind.
   ○ There is a slight breeze.

4. ○ It is cloudy.
   ○ It is sunny.

5. ○ It is quiet outside.
   ○ It is noisy outside.

4. ○ It is stormy.
   ○ It is snowing.

Name ______________________________

Tell About It

Jesus wants us to help others. Think about a time when you helped someone. Draw a picture about it. Write a sentence or two to describe it.

Writing asking and telling sentences

Name ____________________

Ask and Answer

Wow! Jesus has just come to your house. What will you ask him? Write two questions for Jesus. Then write how you think Jesus would answer your questions.

Question

Answer

Question

Answer

How would you feel if Jesus came to your house?

Name ______________________________

You Are Invited

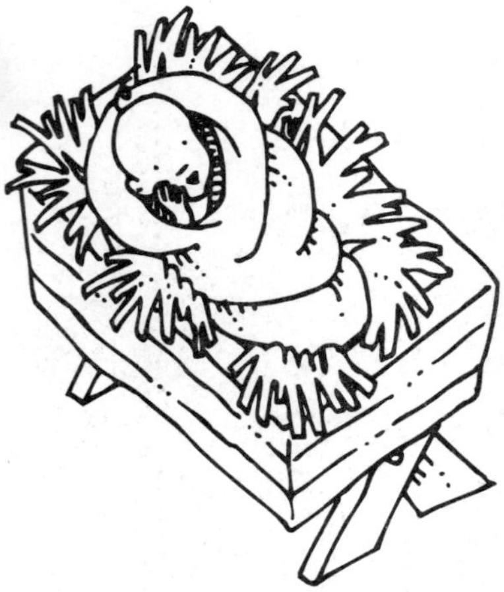

You and the other children at Grace Church are putting on a Christmas play. It will be on Friday, December 22, at 7 p.m. There will be cookies and punch afterward.

Write the invitation.

Please come to our Christmas play.

Date ______________________________

Time ______________________________

Place ______________________________

Put on by ______________________________

Write the title of your play.

____

Name ____________________

Thank You, God

God blesses us in many ways. Think about all the things for which you are thankful. Then write a thank-you note to God.

Dear God,

____

____

____

____

____

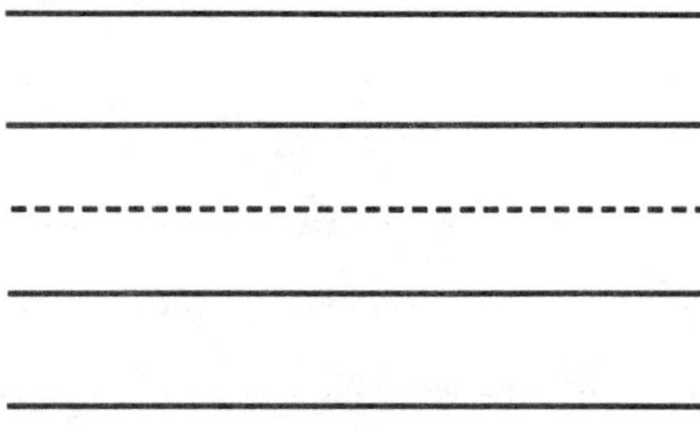

Love,

____

Classifying and categorizing

Name ______________________________

Biblical Groups

Write a new word for each group.

Animals of the Bible

sheep
doves
snakes
donkeys

____

Men in the Bible

Noah
Jonah
Moses
David

____

Jesus' Disciples

Andrew
John
Peter
Matthew

____

Books of the Bible

Genesis
Mark
Psalms
Proverbs

____

Jobs in Bible Times

shepherd
moneychanger
carpenter
farmer

____

Women in the Bible

Ruth
Esther
Mary
Elizabeth

____

Classifying and categorizing

Name ______________________________

Name That Group!

Write a title to name each group of pictures.

1. ______________________________

2. ______________________________

3. ______________________________

4. ______________________________

5. ______________________________

6. ______________________________

7. ______________________________

Name ________________________________

Genesis 6–8

What Happened?

Color the pictures about Noah, the ark, and the flood.
Number the boxes **1**, **2**, **3**, **4**, **5**, and **6** to show the order.

☐ 

☐ 

☐ 

☐ 

☐ 

☐ 

Name ____________________

What's the Effect?

Draw a line to match each set of boxes.

Cause

Ann breaks a lamp but says she didn't do it.

Ann returns a lost wallet.

Ann's family is helping her grandmother do yard work.

Some girls are laughing at Ann's clothes.

Ann's brother broke her favorite toy.

Effect

Ann wants to help.

Ann is upset.

Ann is angry.

Ann feels bad inside.

Ann feels good inside.

Visual discrimination

Name ______________________________

Why Did Jesus Come?

To find the answer to the question above, use the code below. The answer is straight from the mouth of Jesus!

A = ❁	G = ❄	M = ❍	T = ✞
C = ☆	H = ✽	N = ▲	U = ◆
D = ✝	I = ❤	O = ♣	V = ■
E = ❖	K = ◗	R = ✔	Y = ✘
F = ➶	L = ✿	S = ✏	

"... ___
❤

___ ___ ___ ___ ___ ___ ___ ___
✽ ❁ ■ ❖ ☆ ♣ ❍ ❖

___ ___ ___ ___ ___ ___ ___ ___ ___ ___ ___
✞ ✽ ❁ ✞ ✞ ✽ ❖ ✘ ❍ ❁ ✘

___ ___ ___ ___ ___ ___ ___ ___, ___ ___ ___
✽ ❁ ■ ❖ ✿ ❤ ➶ ❖ ❁ ▲ ✝

___ ___ ___ ___ ___ ___ ___ ___ ___ ___ ___
✽ ❁ ■ ❖ ❤ ✞ ✞ ♣ ✞ ✽ ❖

___ ___ ___ ___." (John 10:10b)
➶ ◆ ✿ ✿

Read John 10:1–18 and find out how Jesus used sheep to tell about why He came.

Name ______________________________

Luke 17:11–19

Don't Forget to Thank Jesus

One day, on the road to Jerusalem, some men with leprosy begged Jesus to heal them. He did! But guess what? Not all of the healed men thanked him. Use the color guide below to find out how many thanked him and how many forgot.

• = red •• = yellow
••• = blue

This number remembered to thank him:

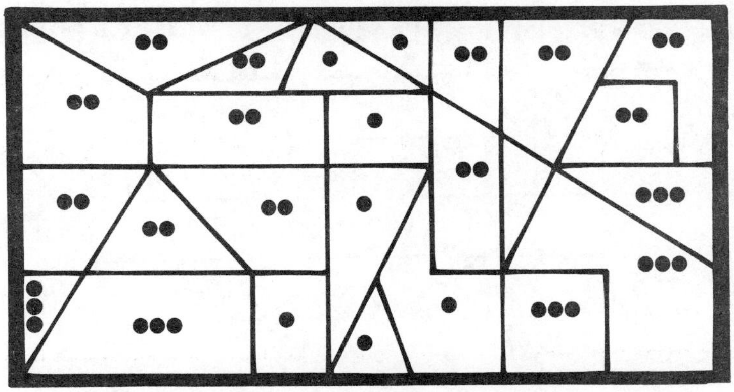

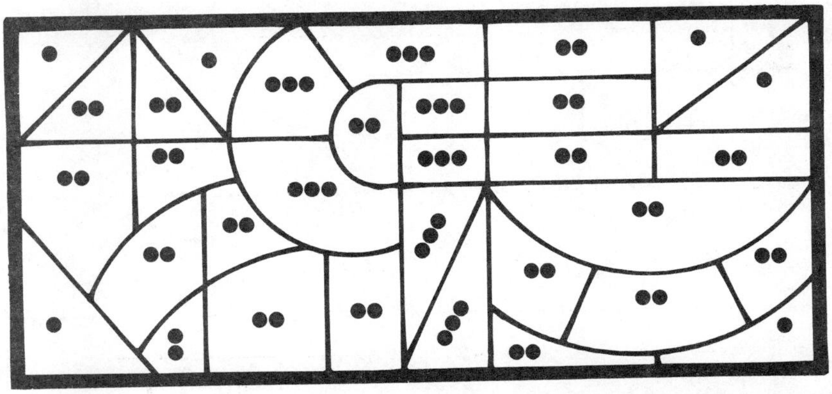

This number forgot to thank him:

This number should be the number of days you forget to thank Jesus for all he does for you!

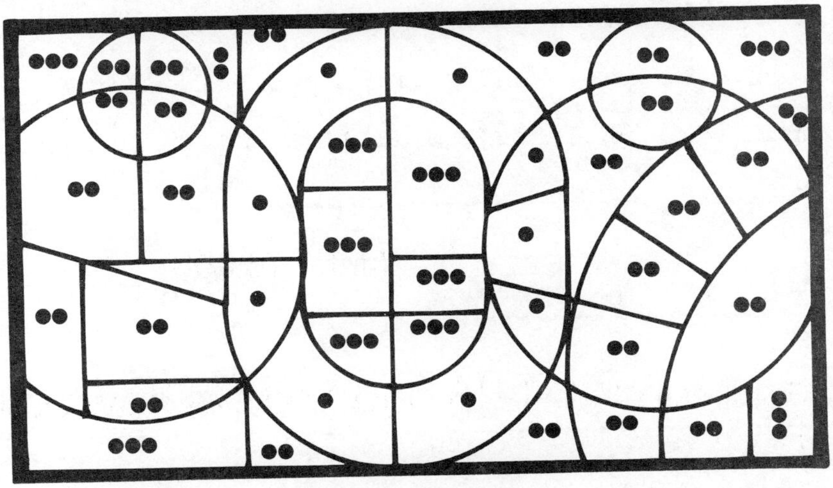

Visual discrimination

Name ______________________________

Matthew 18:11–14

With the Shepherd

Journey with the lamb through the maze to find the Good Shepherd. Match the letters you pass with the lamb to find the missing word in the sentence.

With the Shepherd, you are never

Visual discrimination/
Critical thinking

Name ______________________________

The Main Theme

Follow the directions to find out what the main theme of the Bible is.

Cross out every "A."   Cross out every "B."

Cross out every "L."   Cross out every "Z."

Write the letters that are left in order on the lines under the puzzle.

A	Z	J	L	Z	E
B	S	A	B	U	L
Z	B	S	Z	A	C
A	H	L	R	Z	B
I	Z	L	S	A	T

___ ___ ___ ___ ___   ___ ___ ___ ___ ___ ___

Visual discrimination/
Research

Name ______________________________

Bible Books Word Search

Look at the table of contents in your Bible. Count how many books have only four letters in their names. Write the names on the lines below. Then look for and circle those names in the word search. (Hint: There are nine names—four from the Old Testament and five from the New Testament.)

____

____

____

____

____

____

____

____

____

R	U	T	H	E	Z	R
J	Z	A	R	Z	B	J
U	C	M	A	R	K	O
D	L	O	G	A	J	H
E	U	S	K	L	M	N
O	K	J	O	E	L	Q
T	E	V	A	C	T	S

Name ____________________

Exodus
1 and 2

A Baby in a Basket

Once there was a king. He was mean to the Israelites. He said all the baby Israelite boys should die. An Israelite woman had a baby boy, Moses. She hid him from the king. She made a special basket. She put the baby in it. She put it in the river. The princess found the baby. He went to live in the palace.

Answer the questions.

1. Who was the king mean to?

2. Who did the king want to die?

3. How did the Israelite woman save her baby?

4. What did the woman make?

5. Where did the woman put the basket?

6. Who found the baby?

Name ______________________________

1 Samuel 3

A Voice in the Night

Hannah had a son named Samuel. Samuel went to live with Eli. He would learn to do God's work. One night, Samuel heard a voice call his name three times. He thought it was Eli. Finally, Eli told Samuel that God was calling to him. Samuel listened to God. Samuel became God's messenger.

Complete the puzzle.

Across

2. How many times did God call to Samuel?
5. What was Hannah's son's name?
6. Who called to Samuel?

Down

1. Samuel became what for God?
3. What was the name of Samuel's mother?
4. Who did Samuel go live with?

Name ______________________________

Luke 1

A Special Visit

One day, an angel visited Mary. His name was Gabriel. Gabriel told Mary not to be afraid. He said God loved her. God was going to give Mary a baby. He would be God's son. Mary was to name him Jesus.

1. Fill in the circles if the words tell about the story.

   ○ Gabriel ○ Joseph ○ daughter

   ○ angel ○ Jesus ○ Mary

2. What was God going to give Mary?

   ____

3. What was Mary to name her baby?

   ____

4. Number the events of the story in order.

   _____ God was going to give Mary a baby.

   _____ An angel told Mary not to be afraid.

   _____ Mary was to name her baby Jesus.

   _____ Mary's baby would be God's son.

Name ______________________________

Mark 2:1–12

Jesus Heals a Paralyzed Man

H	E	A	L	E	D
T	F	N	K	M	A
H	O	U	S	E	U
F	U	R	S	A	M
A	R	O	O	F	H
W	A	L	K	E	A

One day, Jesus was teaching in a house. The house was full of people. Four men brought their sick friend to see Jesus. They could not get into the house. The men lowered their friend through the roof. Jesus told the sick man, "Get up and walk." The man was healed.

Write the answers. Circle them in the word search.

1. Where was Jesus teaching? ________________
2. How many men brought their friend to see Jesus? ______
3. The men lowered their friend through what? ___________
4. Jesus told the man to get up and ___________.
5. Jesus ___________ the man.

Name ______________________________

The Animals Came Two by Two

After Noah built the ark, the animals came two by two.
Count by twos. Write the numbers.

Name ______________________________

God Created the Land and the Sky

Write an addition sentence.

1. 

   __4__ + __2__ = ______

2. 

   ______ + ______ = ______

3. 

   ______ + ______ = ______

4. 

   ______ + ______ = ______

5. 

   ______ + ______ = ______

6. 

   ______ + ______ = ______

7. 

   ______ + ______ = ______

8. 

   ______ + ______ = ______

9. 

   ______ + ______ = ______

10. 

    ______ + ______ = ______

Name ______________________________

Adding Up Bible Names

Count the number of letters in each Bible name. Then add the total number of letters in each Bible name to get each answer.

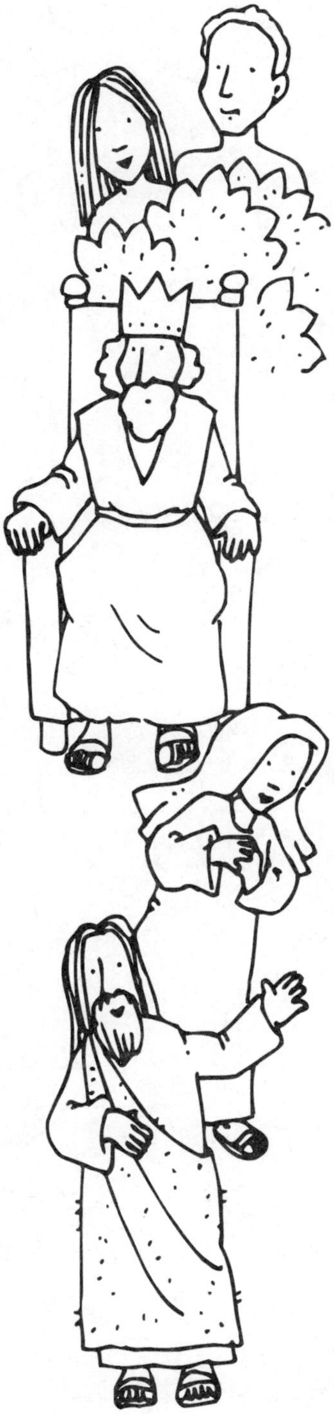

1. Adam + Eve   4 + 3 = 7
2. King Saul + Goliath   8 + 7 = ______
3. Esau + Jacob   ______
4. Moses + Aaron   ______
5. Joseph + Jacob   ______
6. Matthew + Andrew   ______
7. Ruth + Boaz   ______
8. David + Jonathan   ______
9. Abraham + Isaac   ______
10. Barnabas + Bathsheba   ______
11. Mark + Luke   ______
12. Mary + Joseph   ______

Adding two-digit numbers without regrouping

Name ____________________

Praise God With Music

Psalm 33 says, *"Sing joyfully to the Lord . . . Praise the Lord with the harp, make music to him on the ten-stringed lyre . . . play skillfully, and shout for joy."*

Add the numbers in each musical instrument.

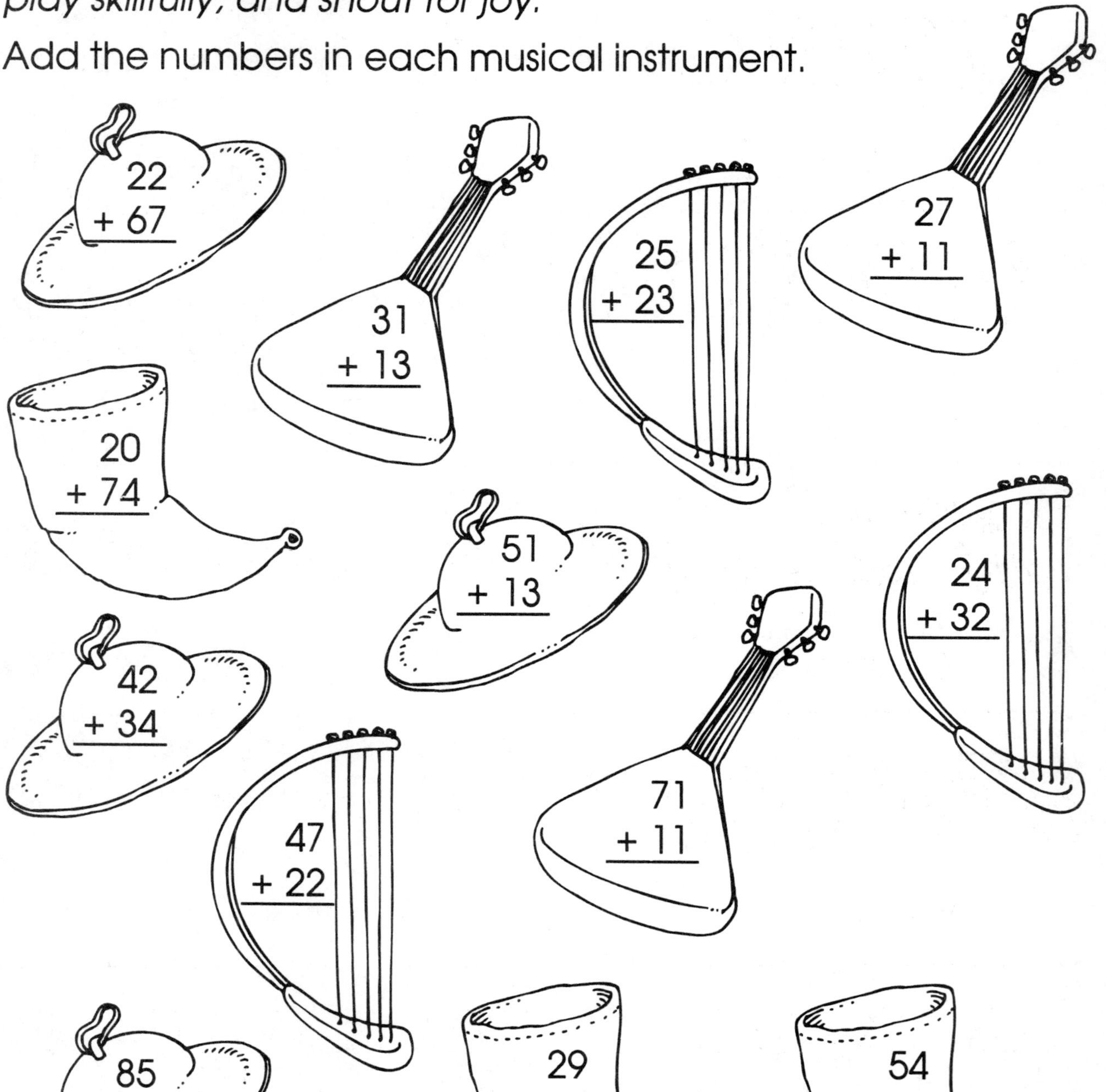

Name ______________________________

God Makes Things Grow

Cross out. Write how many are left.

1.

$5 - 3 =$ 2

2.

$6 - 2 =$ ______

3.

$4 - 1 =$ ______

4.

$5 - 2 =$ ______

5.

$7 - 4 =$ ______

6.

$6 - 5 =$ ______

7.

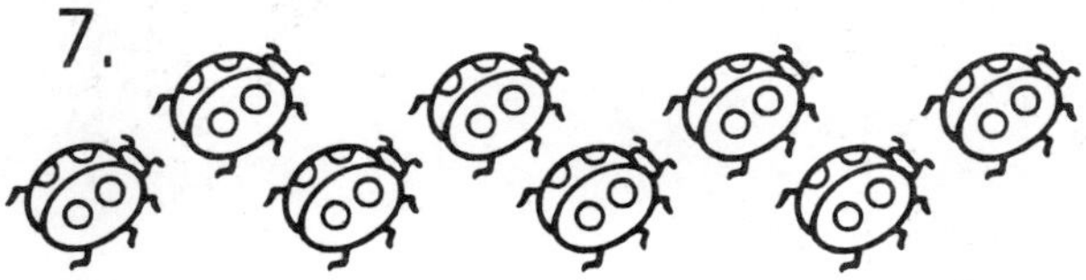

$8 - 8 =$ ______

8.

$7 - 2 =$ ______

9.

$9 - 6 =$ ______

10.

$8 - 4 =$ ______

Name ____

John 2:1–12

From Water to Wine

Jesus went to a wedding in Cana. The wine ran out. There were six water pots. Jesus said to fill them with water. He turned the water into wine.

Solve the subtraction problems below.

$\begin{array}{r} 3 \\ -\ 2 \\ \hline \end{array}$ $\begin{array}{r} 5 \\ -\ 2 \\ \hline \end{array}$ $\begin{array}{r} 13 \\ -\ 3 \\ \hline \end{array}$

$\begin{array}{r} 11 \\ -\ 6 \\ \hline \end{array}$ $\begin{array}{r} 12 \\ -\ 7 \\ \hline \end{array}$ $\begin{array}{r} 9 \\ -\ 7 \\ \hline \end{array}$

9 – 3 = ___ 14 – 5 = ___

7 – 3 = ___ 16 – 7 = ___

6 – 6 = ___ 12 – 4 = ___

8 – 4 = ___ 13 – 7 = ___

17 – 8 = ___

Subtracting two-digit numbers without regrouping

Name ____

A Way to Think of Jesus

Jesus wanted his followers to think of him as the light of something. To find out what it was, solve each problem. Use the key. Write the matching letter in each blank.

59	48	56
− 42	− 24	− 23

"

. . . ____ ____ ____

68	39	98	36	48	88	83
− 58	− 31	− 43	− 12	− 31	− 72	− 12

____ ____ ____ ____ ____   ____ ____

77	67	89	39	29	19	21	87
− 60	− 43	− 56	− 20	− 13	− 19	− 11	− 35

"

____ ____ ____   ____ ____ ____ ____ ____.

A = 20	D = 52	E = 33	F = 71	G = 55	H = 24	I = 8
L = 10	M = 65	O = 16	R = 0	T = 17	W = 19	

Name ______________________________

Pottery Problems

Read the story about the potter. Draw a picture to show the bowls and jars.

The potter had a busy day. First, he made 3 bowls. Then he made 4 big jars. When the clay was dry, he painted a red stripe on 2 bowls and 2 jars. He painted a black stripe on all the other bowls and jars.

Use your picture to solve the problems.

1. How many bowls and jars did the potter make? ______
2. How many more jars than bowls did he make? ______
3. How many bowls and jars have a red stripe? ______
4. How many bowls and jars have a black stripe? ______

Name ______________________________

Unroll the Scroll

In Jesus' time, books called scrolls were made by gluing pieces of papyrus together to make one long roll. Each end was fastened to a stick. The scroll was rolled up.

Find the number patterns on the scroll. Write the missing numbers.

55, 56, ___, 58, 59, ___, 61, ___, ___

20, ___, ___, 50, 60, ___, 80, ___, 100

___, 10, ___, 20, 25, 30, ___, 40, 45, ___

46, 48, 50, 52, ___, 56, ___, ___, 62

100, ___, 300, 400, ___, ___, 700, 800

1, ___, 5, 7, ___, 11, 13, ___, ___, 19

50, 55, ___, ___, 70, ___, ___, ___, 90, ___

Name ________________________________

Count on God

Write the missing numbers in the chart. Then count by fives, and color each fifth square.

	2	3					8		
	12			15		17		19	
21			24				28	29	30
			34		36			39	
	42			45			48		
51				55		57		59	60
		63				67			
	72		74	75				79	
		83		85			88		
91		93				97			

Name ______________________________

Matthew
14:31–21

Two Fish and Five Loaves

One time, Jesus fed more than 5,000 people with two fish and five loaves of bread. Look at each loaf of bread. Answer the questions. Follow the directions.

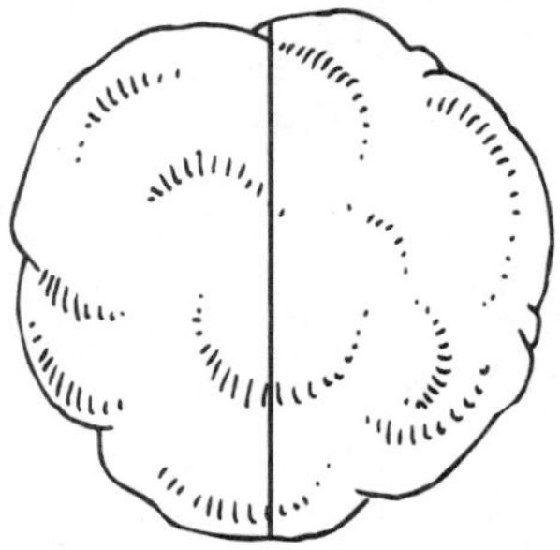

1. How many equal parts are there? __________

Color $\frac{1}{2}$ yellow.

Color $\frac{1}{2}$ orange.

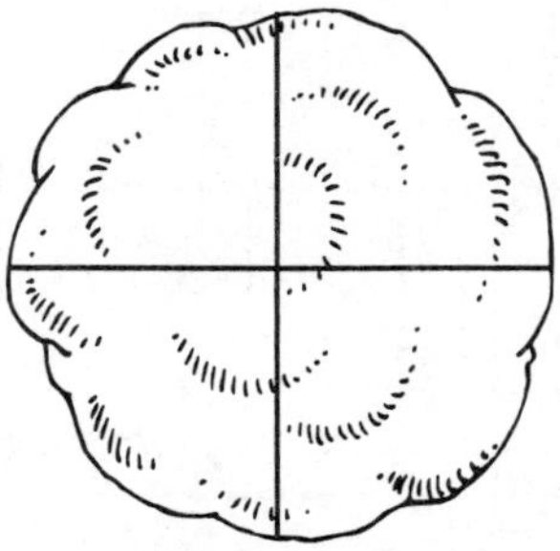

2. How many equal parts are there? __________

Color $\frac{1}{4}$ red.

Color $\frac{3}{4}$ green.

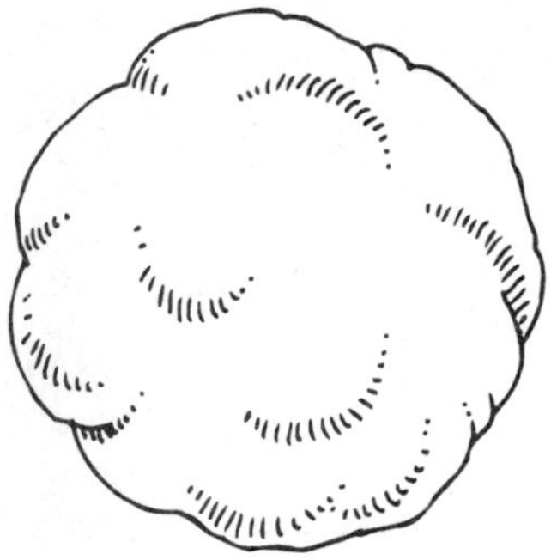

3. How many parts are there? _______

Draw a line to make 2 equal parts. Draw another line to make 4 equal parts.

Color $\frac{1}{2}$ blue. Color $\frac{1}{4}$ purple.

Color $\frac{1}{4}$ brown.

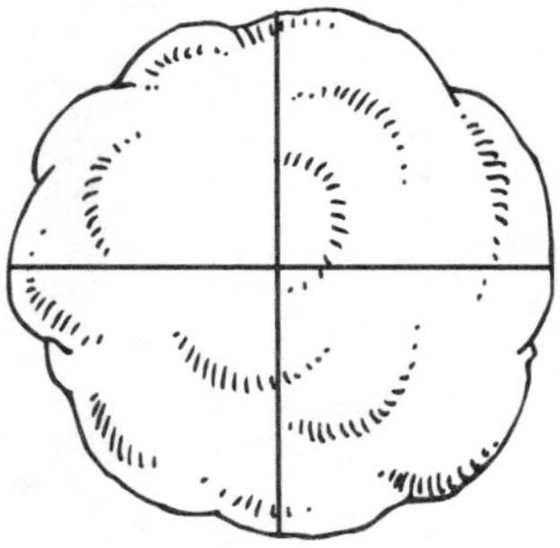

4. How many equal parts are there? _______

Draw 2 lines to make 8 equal parts.

Color $\frac{4}{8}$ blue. Color $\frac{2}{8}$ yellow.

Color $\frac{2}{8}$ green.

Name ______________________________

The Other Half

Draw a part that will match when you fold it on the dotted line.

1.

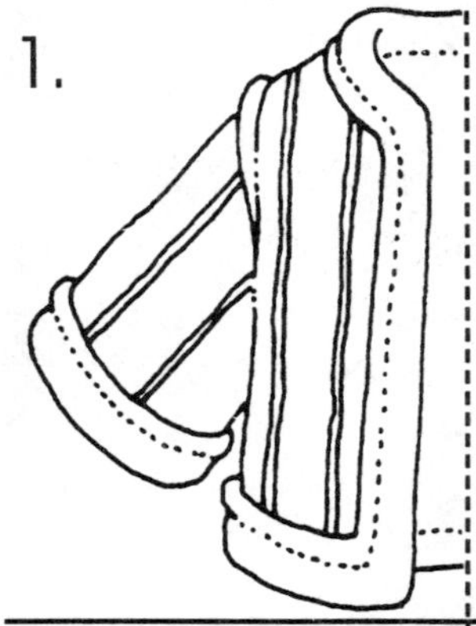

2.

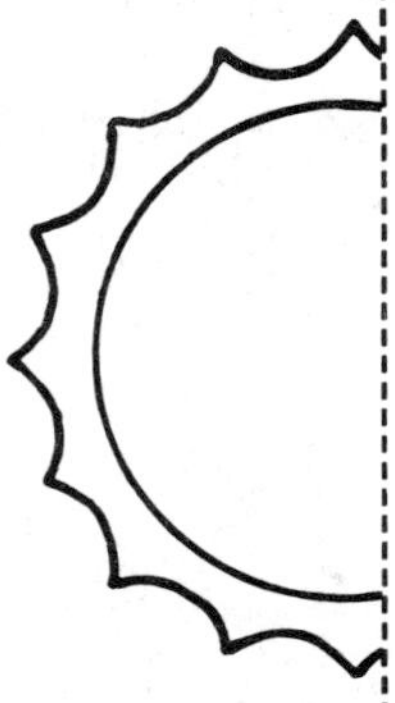

3.

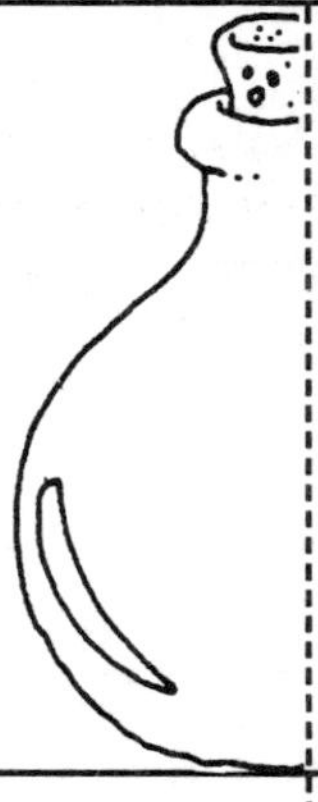

4.

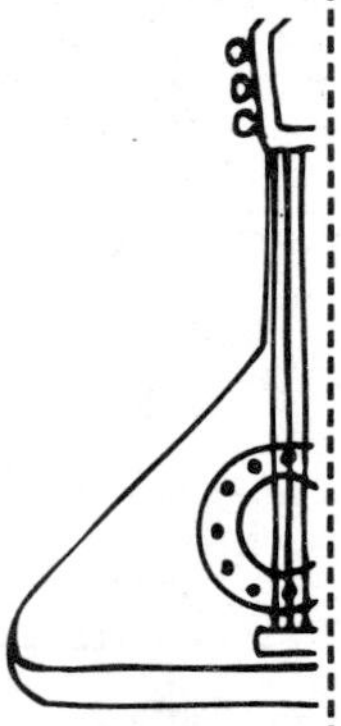

5.

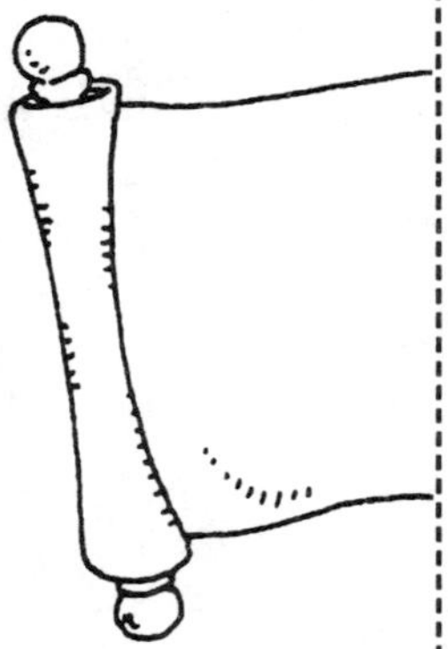

6.

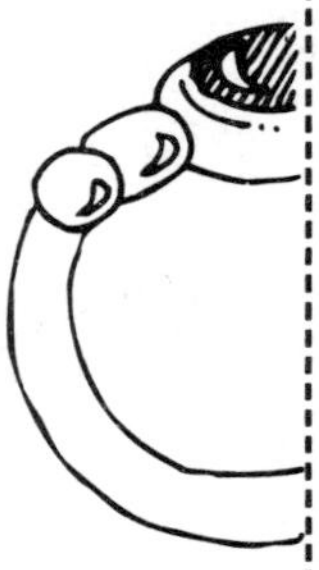

7.

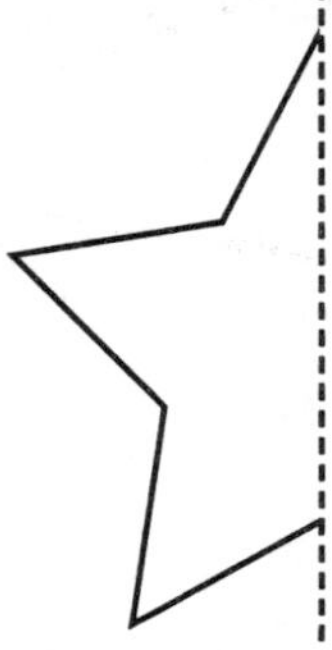

8.

Name ____

Going to Bethlehem

It probably took Mary and Joseph three days to travel by donkey from Nazareth to Bethlehem.

Use an inch ruler to measure the road they took. Mark each inch. Then add to see about how far they traveled.

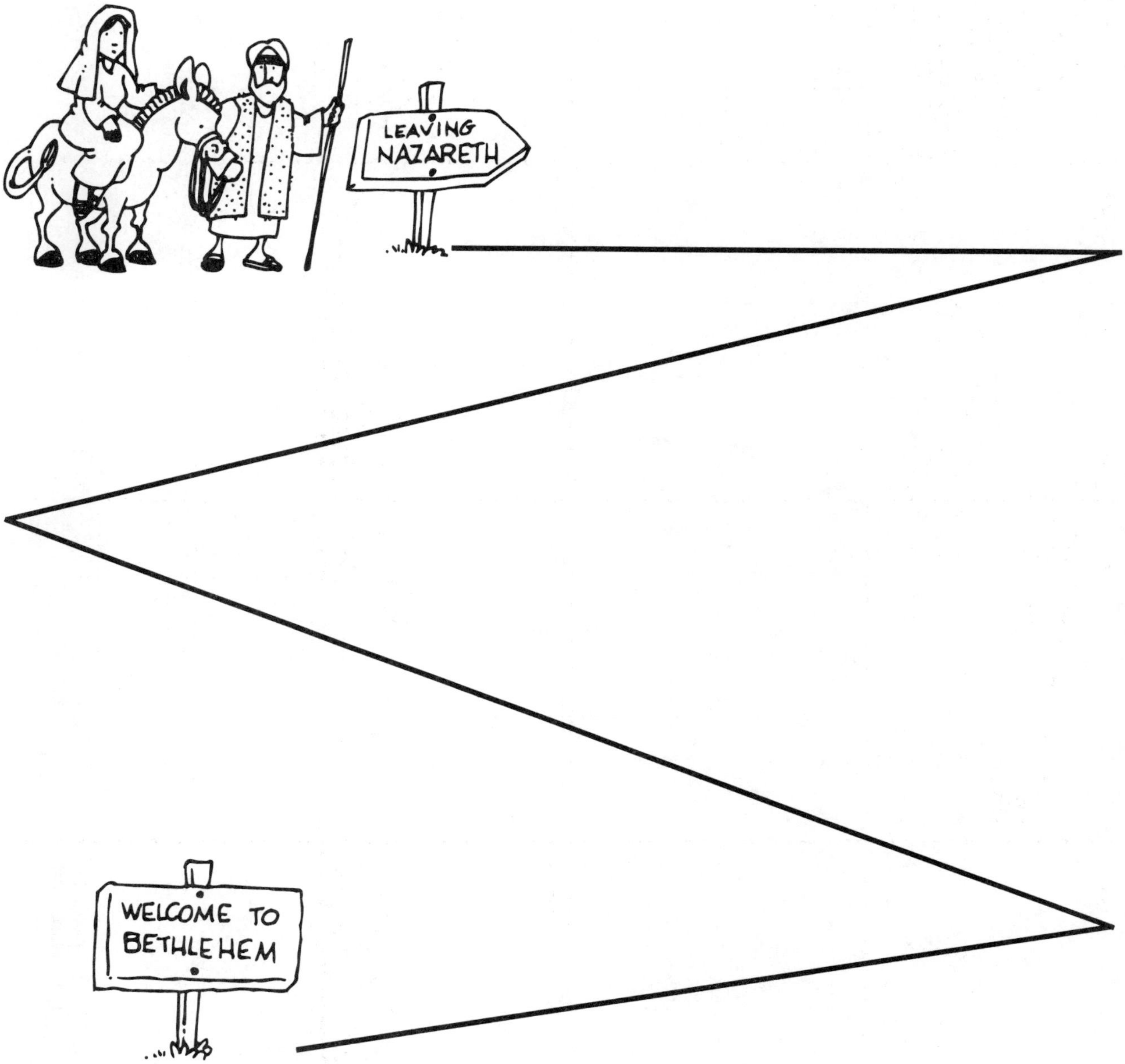

Mary and Joseph traveled about _____ miles.

Name ______________________________

Sarah's Sunday

See how Sarah spent Sunday. Write the time you see on each clock.

____:____

____:____

____:____

____:____

____:____

____:____

Name ______________________________

Saving for the Lord

It is important to share our money with others who need it.

Match.

5¢

10¢

25¢

1¢

Write the amount.

1. ☐ 

2. ☐ 

3. ☐ 

4. ☐ 

5. ☐ 

6. ☐ 

7. ☐ 

8. ☐ 

Name ______________________

Giving to Others

We should make wise choices when we spend our money, and we should always give money to church.

Write the amount of money in each row. Can you buy the object? Write **yes** or **no**.

1.

____
____

2.

____
____

3.

____
____

4.

____
____

5.

____
____

6.

____
____

7.

____
____

Name ____

My Favorite Bible Story

Ask 10 friends this question:

Which Bible story do you like the most—"David and Goliath," "Jonah and the Big Fish," "Noah's Ark," or "Jesus Walking on Water"?

Begin with the bottom box in each column and color a box for each answer.

Favorite Bible Story Graph

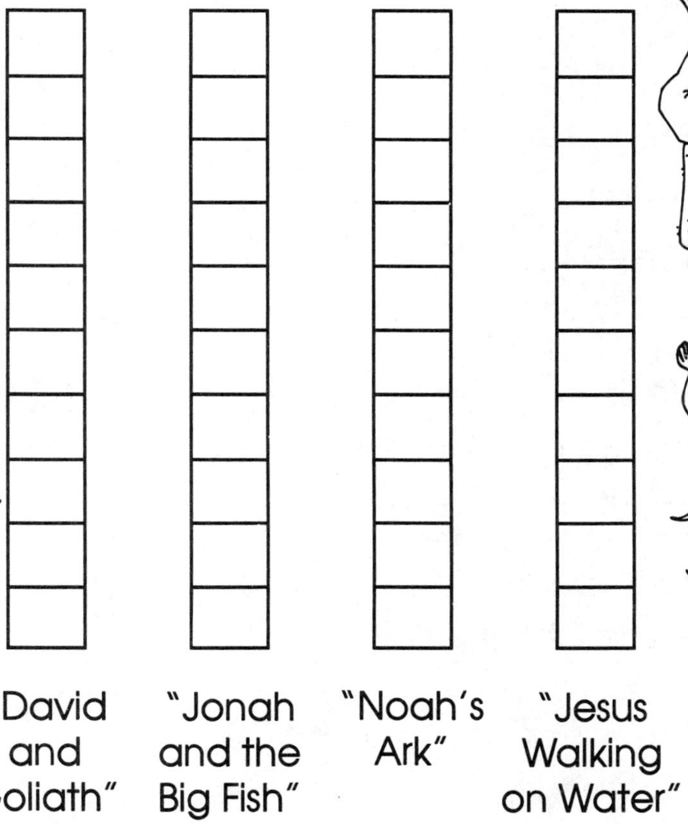

Write the name of your favorite Bible story.

____

____

Name ____________________

"Hunger and Thirst" Banner

"Blessed are those who hunger and thirst for righteousness, for they will be filled." (Matthew 5:6)

Materials Needed:

pattern (page 69)
tagboard
6" x 9" felt (any color)
7 ½" drinking straw
30" piece of yarn
seeds (corn, dried beans, rice) or macaroni
thin-line marker
scissors
glue
stapler (optional)

Figure 1

Directions:

1. Trace around the pattern on tagboard and cut it out.
2. Trace around the pattern on felt. (Use the thin-line marker for this.)
3. On the felt, glue gold or red seeds on the cup and white seeds on the bread. (Figure 1) You may prefer to use colored macaroni.
4. Lightly print the Bible verse, Matthew 5:6, under the cup and bread.
5. Glue small seeds or rice over the letters.
6. Thread the yarn through the drinking straw and tie the ends together at the top to make a hanger. (Figure 2)
7. Fold the top edge of the felt over the straw and glue or staple it in place. (Figure 3)

Figure 2

Figure 3

Name ____________________

"Hunger and Thirst" Banner Pattern

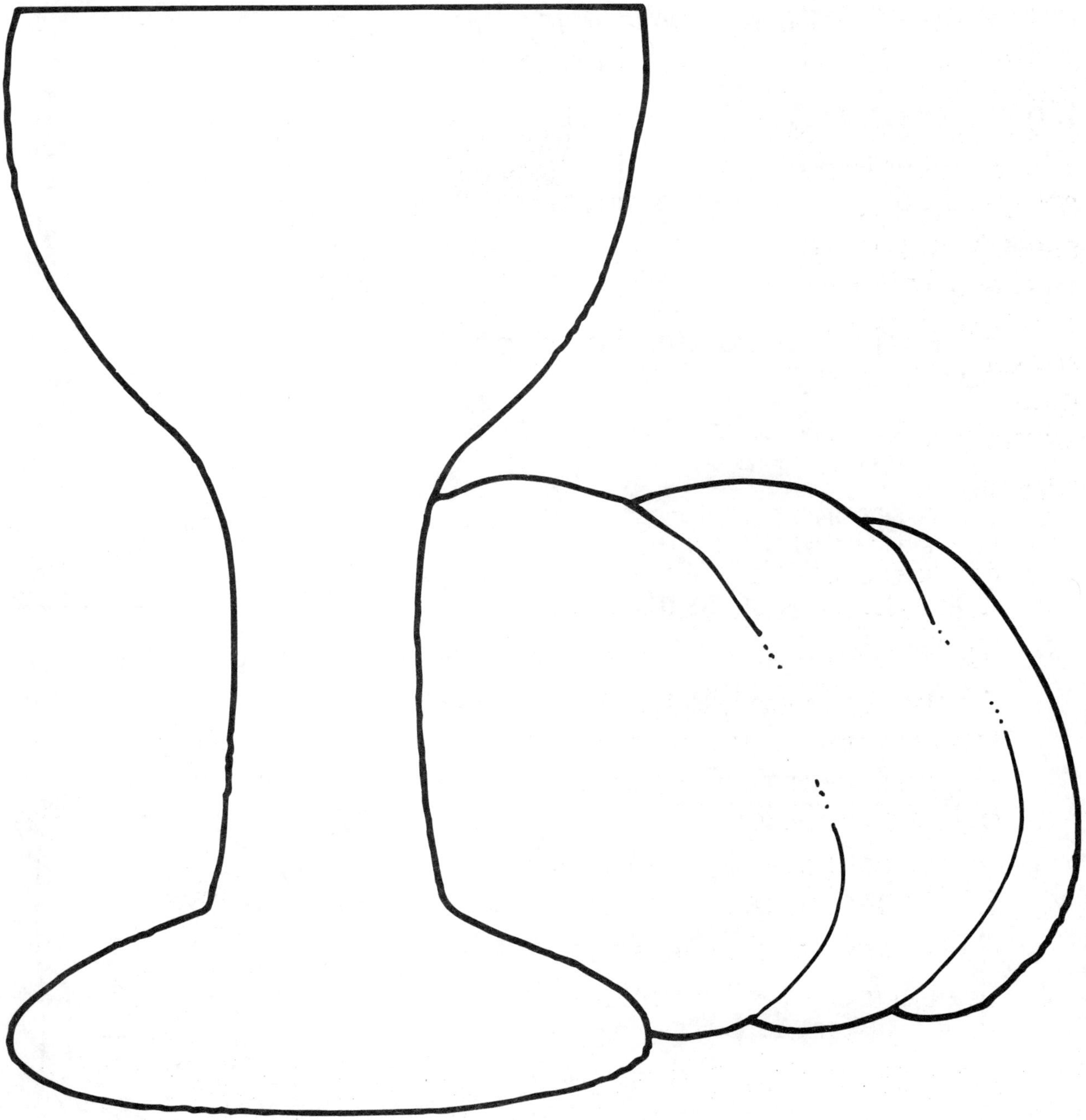

Name ______________________________

Good Samaritan Helping Hands Reminder

"Blessed are the merciful, for they will be shown mercy."
(Matthew 5:7)

Materials Needed:
construction paper
crayons, colored pencils, or markers
scissors

Directions:

1. Fold a sheet of construction paper in half. (Figure 1)
2. Place your hand on the folded paper as shown. (Figure 2)
3. Trace around your hand and cut it out. Do not cut across the fold.
4. Color and decorate the hands.
5. On the inside of the folded hands, write ways you can help and show mercy to other people. (Figure 3)

Figure 1

Figure 2

Figure 3

Name ______________________________

"Inherit the Earth" Garden

"Blessed are the meek, for they will inherit the earth."
(Matthew 5:5)

Materials Needed:

patterns (page 72)
½ gallon milk or juice carton
acrylic paint and brushes
crayons, colored pencils, or markers
craft sticks
potting soil
seeds
scissors
glue

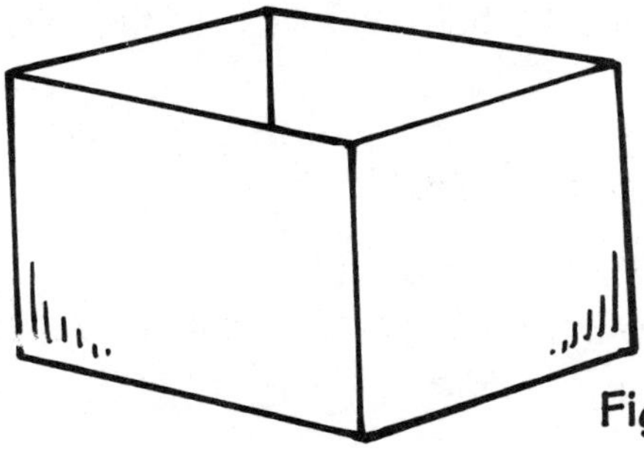

Figure 1

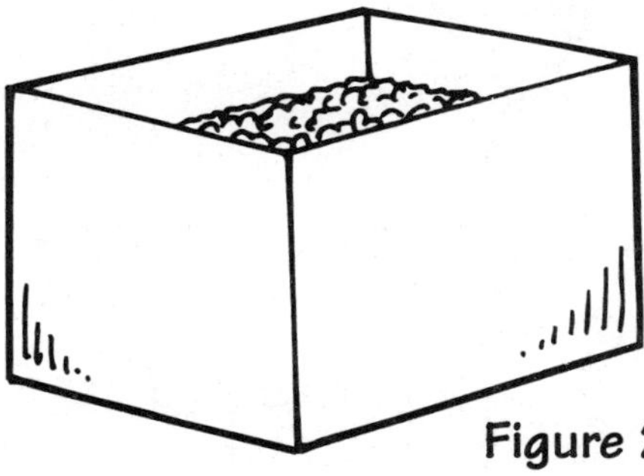

Figure 2

Directions:

1. Cut off the top of the milk or juice carton. (Figure 1) Wash it out with warm, soapy water and rinse it until it's completely clean and not sticky.
2. Paint the carton with acrylic paint. Two coats may be necessary. Allow each coat to dry thoroughly.
3. Fill the carton with potting soil. (Figure 2)
4. Plant seeds in the soil.
5. Place the "garden" in a sunny location and water it when the soil becomes dry.
6. Color and cut out the plant markers from page 72.
7. Glue each marker to a craft stick. (Figure 3)
8. Stick the plant markers into your "garden" and in other potted plants around the house. (Figure 4)

Figure 3

Figure 4

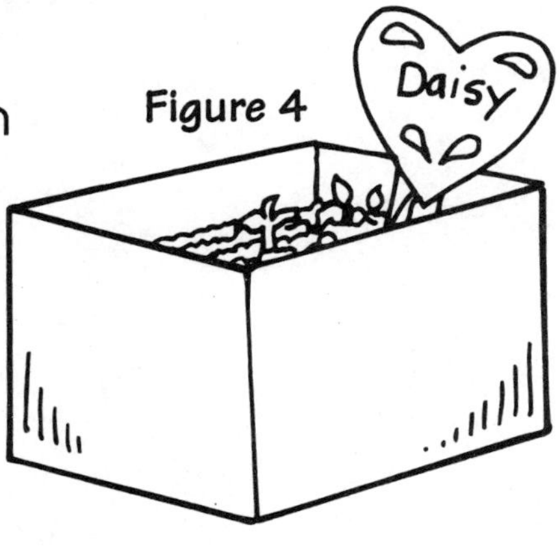

Name ____________________

"Inherit the Earth" Garden Patterns

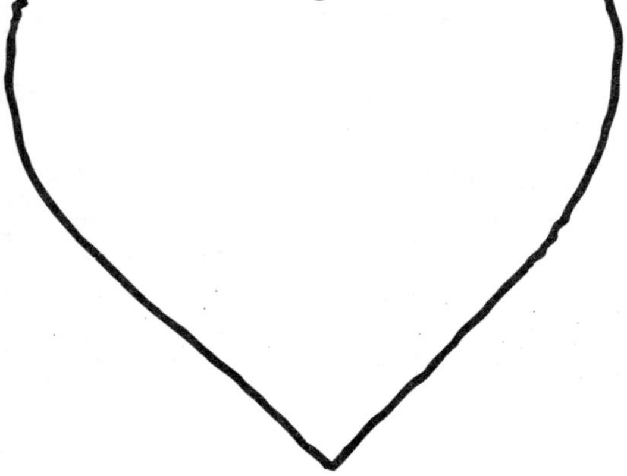

Name ____________________

Fruitful Place Settings

Materials Needed:

plain paper place mats and matching paper napkins
paper cups or clear plastic disposable cups
paper plates or disposable plastic plates
fruit-shaped stickers (or hearts and smiley faces)
crayons, markers, or paint pens

Directions:

1. Decorate a place setting with words, stickers, and designs that will remind everyone what the fruit of the Spirit (Galatians 5:22–23) is. (Do not decorate the inside surfaces where food or drinks will be.)
2. Make several place settings. Make one for each member of your family at mealtime or if you are planning a party, set a place for each guest.

Other Ideas:

- Use paper plates, cups, napkins, place mats, etc., that already have some background fruits printed on them and decorate them with additional stickers.
- Instead of buying place mats, make some from colored construction paper. Snip the edges to make a fringe.
- Glue a collage design on the place mats using pictures of fruits and words cut from magazines and greeting cards.
- Use paint pens to decorate the handles of plastic utensils, such as forks and spoons.
- Decorate clear plastic or glass dishes. They last longer than paper.

Name ____________________

Personal Responsibility Chart

Materials Needed:

copy of the chart on page 75
scissors
markers or reward stickers (fruit shapes, happy faces, stars, etc.)

Directions:

1. Cut out the chart.
2. Each day, try to show the fruit of the Spirit (Galatians 5:22–23) in your attitude and actions. Write on the chart how you can do this. Mark each one off as you do it with a check mark, by coloring in the square, or by putting a sticker in the square for the day. Make it your own responsibility to fill out your chart without being reminded.

Other Ideas:

- Discuss with others what it means to practice self-control to follow a plan every day and do what God wants.
- Make a Daily Chores Chart and put it on your refrigerator at home. Your parents will be proud of you and glad that they don't have to remind you to do your chores.
- Make a personal chart or keep a private diary of your progress in areas requiring self-control. (Examples: watching only a certain amount of television, doing your homework before going outside to play, not eating sweet snacks before dinner, brushing your teeth without being reminded)
- Fill in the squares on the chart using ink stamps or fruit-scented pens or crayons.

Name ______________________________

Personal Responsibility Chart

	How I Can Show It:	Sunday	Monday	Tuesday	Wednesday	Thursday	Friday	Saturday
Love								
Joy								
Peace								
Patience								
Kindness								
Goodness								
Faithfulness								
Gentleness								
Self-Control								

Name ______________________________

"Welcome Friends" Doorknob Hanger

Materials Needed:

doorknob hanger pattern
colored posterboard
scissors
colored markers
stickers (fruits, hearts, tiny cottages, etc.)

Directions:

1. Trace around the doorknob hanger pattern on posterboard.
2. Cut it out.
3. Decorate the hanger with stickers and draw pictures on it. Print on it these words: "Welcome Friends!"
4. Hang the doorknob hanger on your front door, the door to your room, or give it to someone as a gift.

Other Ideas:

- Buy a pre-cut doorknob hanger pattern at a craft or hobby store. Paint it and glue on wooden decorations. Write on it with enamel paint pens.
- Cut the pattern out of lightweight cardboard and cover it with colored construction paper or colored plastic adhesive.

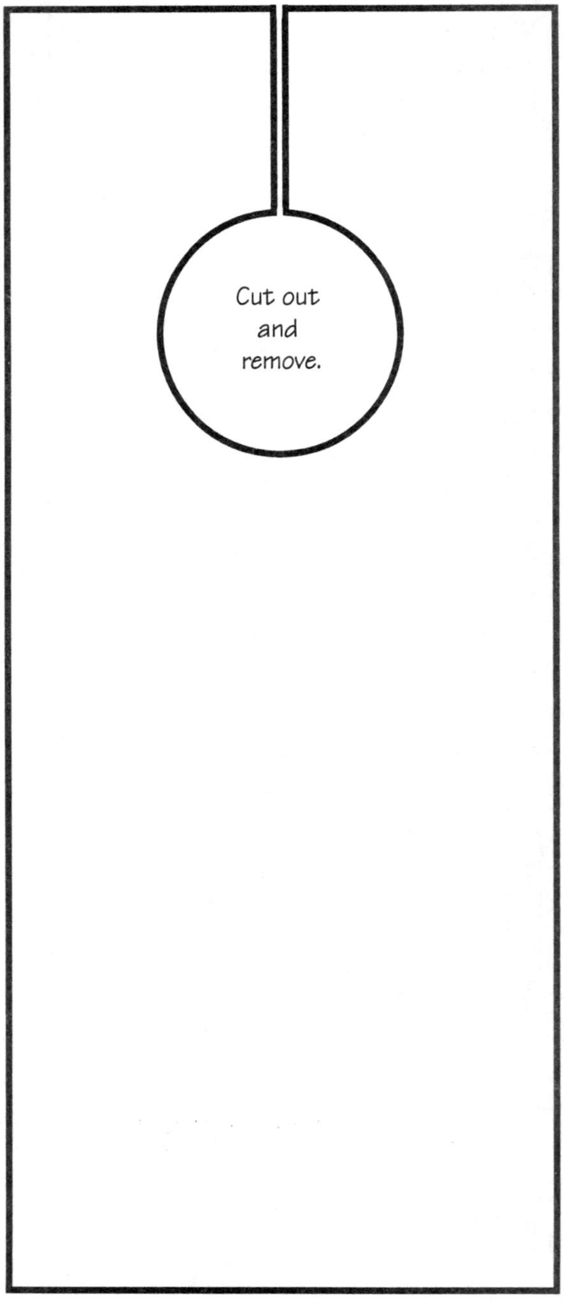

Answers

Page 2

1. b	2. l	3. w
4. m	5. d	6. t
7. n	8. h	9. s
10. r	11. f	12. c
13. b	14. s	15. b

Page 3

1. tent, turtle
2. lamp, lamb
3. basket, bowl
4. rainbow, river
5. camel, cave
6. men, mountain
7. star, sun

Page 4

"You will find a baby wrapped in cloths and lying in a manger."

Page 5

Jesus is the light of the world!

Page 6

1. **cr**oss	2. **pr**ay
3. **cr**own	4. **gr**apes
5. **tr**umpet	6. **fr**og
7. **br**ead	8. **br**anch
9. **fr**iends	10. **tr**ee
11. **dr**um	12. **tr**unk

Page 7

1. **sh**eep	2. **ch**urch
3. **sh**ip	4. **th**orn
5. **sh**ell	6. **ch**ildren

c	h	i	l	d	r	e	n	t
h	c	h	i	y	n	s	s	x
u	s	h	c	h	t	h	h	r
r	h	t	h	o	r	n	e	w
c	i	s	c	t	h	s	e	e
h	p	s	h	e	l	l	p	c

Page 8

1. sun	2. hand	3. fish
4. net	5. pot	6. cat
7. hug	8. lamp	9. hill
10. bell	11. fox	12. lips

Page 9

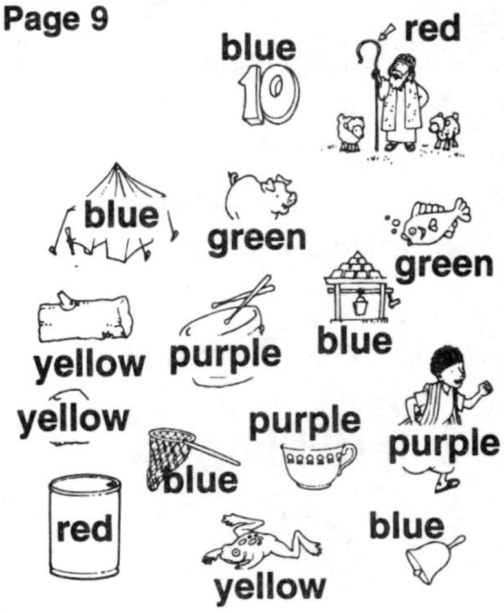

Page 10

1. robe	2. flute
3. knife	4. stone
5. gate	6. bike
7. smile	8. mule
9. lake	10. rope
11. vine	12. time

Page 11

1. calf	2. **k**neel
3. si**g**n	4. clim**b**
5. s**w**ord	6. **w**rite
7. lam**b**	8. wa**l**k
9. mi**gh**ty	10. **w**rist
11. **k**nife	12. lim**b**

Page 12

1. well	2. dish	3. save
4. day	5. dark	6. love
7. feed	8. calf	9. coat
10. went	11. pan	12. peep

Page 13

1. huge	2. afraid
3. large, huge	4. small
5. brave	6. lifted
7. struck	8. glad

Page 14

1. old	2. love	3. well
4. far	5. right	6. light

Page 15

every/thing	in/side
every/one	rain/bow

Page 16

Fish should be colored according to directions.

Page 17

1. lamp	2. cross
3. camel	4. bread
5. twelve	6. sling
7. well	8. boat
9. star	10. kiss
11. sheep	12. Bible

Page 18

1. Jesus and the disciples were in a boat.
2. A storm came up.
3. The disciples thought they might sink.
4. Jesus asked why they were afraid.
5. He told the wind and the sea to be quiet and calm.

Page 19

1. The children are learning about Jesus.
2. Dan is reading his Bible.
3. Martha is singing in church.
4. Cal is talking to God.
5. The pastor is talking about Jesus.

Page 20

Maggie wants to learn about Jesus.
Alex knows many things about Jesus.
Answers will vary.

Page 21

1. Jesus and Jairus' Daughter
2. John Mark
3. Mary Miller
4. Answers will vary.

Page 22

Nineveh, bad, good, storm, sea, whale, prayed, spit

Page 23

Answers will vary.

Answers

Page 24

Mary and Joseph lived in the town of Nazareth in a country called Palestine. The ruler wanted to count everyone in his empire. To do this, people were ordered to go back to their hometowns. Mary and Joseph returned to Bethlehem. It was there that baby Jesus was born.

Names of People: Jesus, Joseph, Mary

Names of Places: Bethlehem, Nazareth, Palestine

Answers will vary.

Page 25

1. babies
2. church
3. angels
4. cities
5. lamb
6. crosses
7. Bibles

Page 26

y sounds like **e**: army, baby, city

y sounds like **i**: sky, cry, fly

Answers will vary.

Page 27

1. Jesus
2. Noah
3. David
4. Adam
5. Eve
6. Moses
7. Jonah

Page 28

1. A man sat by the road.
2. He needed help.
3. He could not see.
4. Jesus walked by.
5. Jesus made him see.
6. The man was happy.

Page 29

1. **.**
2. **.**
3. **?**
4. **.**
5. **?**
6. **?**
7. **.**
8. **.**
9. **?**
10. **.**

Page 30

Answers will vary.

Page 31

Answers will vary.

Page 32

1. Child circles middle picture.
2. Child circles first picture.
3. Child circles first picture.
4. Child circles middle picture.
5. Child circles last picture.

Page 33

1. It has stopped raining.
2. It is warm.
3. There is a strong wind.
4. It is cloudy.
5. It is noisy outside.
6. It is stormy.

Page 34

Answers will vary.

Page 35

Answers will vary.

Page 36

Please come to our Christmas play.

Date **December 22**

Time **7:00 p.m.**

Place **Grace Church**

Put on by **children**

Page 37

Answers will vary.

Page 38

Answers will vary. Possible responses are as follows:

Animals of the Bible: camels, frogs, goats, fish

Jesus' Disciples: James, Philip, Bartholomew, Thomas, Simon, Thaddaeus, Judas, James

Jobs in Bible Times: baker, fisherman, gatekeeper, innkeeper, judge, lawyer, maid, musician, nurse

Men in the Bible: Goliath, Adam, Abraham, Esau, Jacob

Books of the Bible: There are 66.

Women in the Bible: Miriam, Deborah, Hannah, Martha

Page 39

1. Clothing
2. Tools
3. Trees
4. Boats
5. Insects/Bugs
6. Foods
7. Animals

Page 40

5, 3; 2, 4; 6, 1

Page 41

Page 42

". . . I have come that they may have life, and have it to the full."

Page 43

1; 9; 0

Page 44

lost

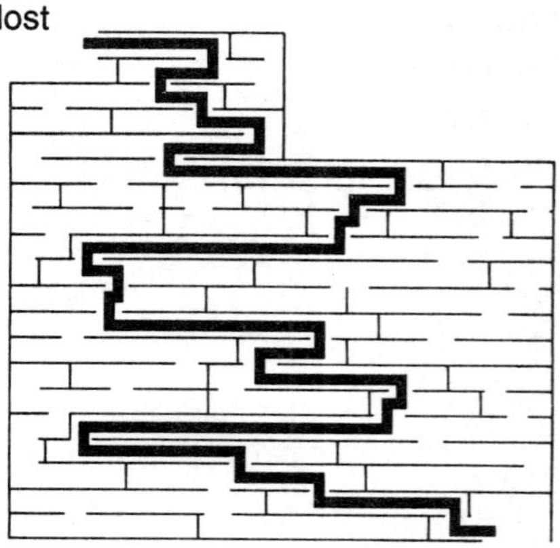

Page 45

Jesus Christ

Answers

Page 46

Ruth, Mark, Acts, John, Luke, Jude, Ezra, Joel, Amos

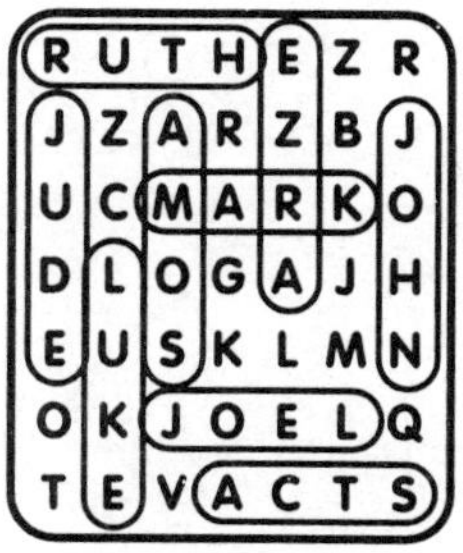

Page 47

1. the Israelites
2. baby Israelite boys
3. She hid him from the king.
4. a special basket
5. in the river
6. the princess

Page 48

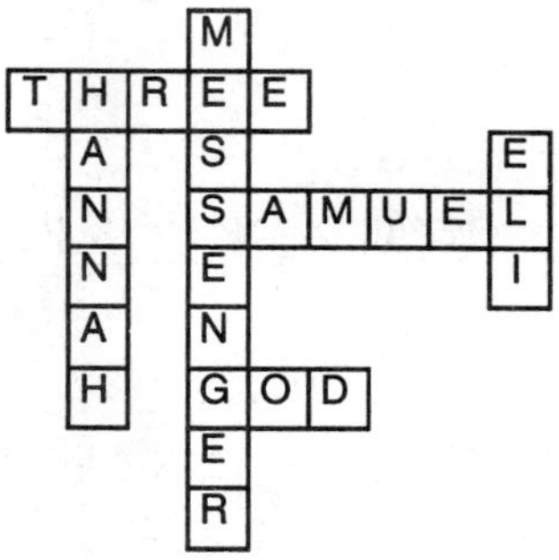

Page 49

1. Gabriel, angel, Jesus, Mary
2. a baby
3. Jesus
4. going from left to right: 2, 1, 4, 3

Page 50

1. house
2. four
3. roof
4. walk
5. healed

Page 51

2, 4, 6, 8, 10, 12, 14, 16, 18, 20, 22, 24, 26, 28, 30, 32, 34, 36, 38, 40, 42, 44, 46, 48, 50

Page 52

1. 4 + 2 = 6
2. 1 + 2 = 3
3. 3 + 3 = 6
4. 4 + 3 = 7
5. 2 + 5 = 7
6. 5 + 1 = 6
7. 4 + 4 = 8
8. 5 + 4 = 9
9. 2 + 6 = 8
10. 3 + 2 = 5

Page 53

1. 4 + 3 = 7
2. 8 + 7 = 15
3. 4 + 5 = 9
4. 5 + 5 = 10
5. 6 + 5 = 11
6. 7 + 6 = 13
7. 4 + 4 = 8
8. 5 + 8 = 13
9. 7 + 5 = 12
10. 8 + 9 = 17
11. 4 + 4 = 8
12. 4 + 6 = 10

Page 54

Page 55

1. 2
2. 4
3. 3
4. 3
5. 3
6. 1
7. 0
8. 5
9. 3
10. 4

Page 56

Page 57

". . . the light of the world."

Page 58

1. 7
2. 1
3. 4
4. 3

Page 59

57, 60, 62, 63
30, 40, 70, 90
5, 15, 35, 50
54, 58, 60
200, 500, 600
3, 9, 15, 17
60, 65, 75, 80, 85, 95

Page 60

Check child's answers.

Page 61

1. 2
2. 4
3. 1
4. 4

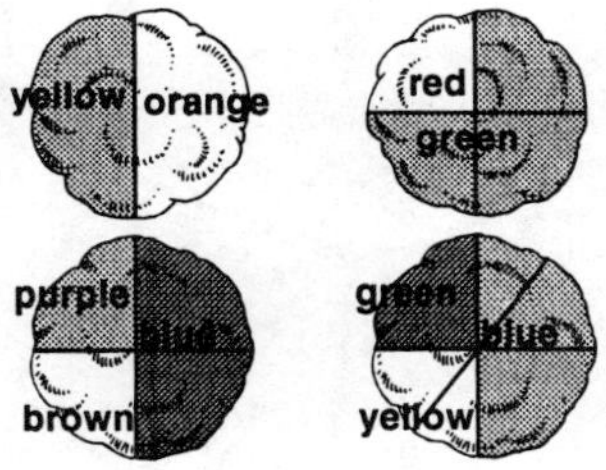

Page 62

Check child's drawings.

Page 63

23 miles

Page 64

7:00, 9:00, 10:00, 12:00, 6:00, 8:00

Page 65

1. 10¢
2. 11¢
3. 6¢
4. 35¢
5. 31¢
6. 25¢
7. 22¢
8. 50¢

Page 66

1. 73¢, yes
2. $1.15, yes
3. 68¢, no
4. $1.02, yes
5. $1.32, yes
6. $1.00, no
7. 85¢, yes

Page 67

Answers will vary.

Name

Loves God and is Super Smart!

Presented by

Date